L is for Lobster

A Maine Alphabet

LIBRARY
FRANKLIN PIERCE COLLEGE
RINDGE NH 03461

Written by Cynthia Furlong Reynolds and Illustrated by Jeannie Brett

Text Copyright © 2001 Cynthia Furlong Reynolds
Illustrations Copyright © 2001 Jeannie Brett

Permission for and reference material used to illustrate Leon Leonwood Bean for the
letter B provided by L.L. Bean, Inc..

All rights reserved. No part of this book may be reproduced in any manner without the
express written consent of the publisher, except in the case of brief excerpts in critical
reviews and articles. All inquiries should be addressed to:

Sleeping Bear Press
310 North Main Street
P.O. Box 20
Chelsea, MI 48118
www.sleepingbearpress.com

Printed and bound in Canada

10 9 8 7 6 5 4 3 2 1

Library of Congress Cataloging-in-Publication Data on file.
ISBN: 1-58536-024-4

CURR
F9.3
.R49
2001

D is for Dedication

This book is dedicated to Mrs. Tupper,
Who asked me to write a book like this long ago,

And to the Furlongs, Spragues, Stinsons, Shaws, Smalls, Leightons, Henleys,
and Knowltons who planted my roots in the rocky soil of Maine generations ago,

And to my family,who watered those roots and encouraged them to grow.

CYNTHIA

For my mother.

JEANNIE

A stands for Augusta,
the capital of our state.
In the rooms of the statehouse,
our representatives legislate.

To legislate means to make and vote on laws. We have 35 Senators and 151 members of the House of Representatives working in Augusta to make the laws for our state. Augusta is also where Maine's governor lives, in The Blaine House.

In 1628, Pilgrims built a trading post on the Kennebec River where Augusta now stands. More than 100 years later, Fort Western was built on the same spot. It wasn't until 1797 that the city surrounding the fort was named Augusta, in honor of the daughter of Revolutionary War hero Henry Dearborn. Although Maine separated from Massachusetts to become the 23rd state in the Union in 1820, it wasn't until 1827 that Augusta was named the capital.

Early Pilgrim and Puritan settlers would put a pot of beans in the fire on Saturday morning and bake them all day long. Because they were delicious, nutritious, and easy to bake, beans and brown bread quickly became the traditional Saturday night meal in Maine.

B&M stands for Burnham & Morrill. They have been baking and canning beans in Portland since 1900. Every week 1,575 pots of beans are baked in brick ovens.

Leon Leonwood Bean, a Maine outdoorsman, founded L.L. Bean in 1912. He was tired of cold, wet feet, so he invented a new kind of boot and began selling his design by mail to other sportsmen. By 1917, he had so many customers stopping by his shop that he decided to open a showroom along with his mail order catalog business. Today, the L.L. Bean store in Freeport, Maine is open 24 hours a day, 365 days a year.

B b

B is for Beans—
B&M and L.L.
One bakes food you can eat,
the other has goods to sell.

The Native Americans called the chickadee "bird of the happy heart" because the chickadee loves to sing.

Chickadees are robed in gray and white, with buff-colored feathers and a black feather cap and bib. The male and female build their nest together in rock walls or low-lying tree branches. The nest is made of thistle down, horsehair, small reeds, cotton from the cottonwood trees, and other soft materials. The mother bird lays as many as eight small white eggs, with reddish-brown spots. Then she sits in her soft nest over the eggs for 12 days until the babies hatch. For the next two weeks, both parents are kept busy trying to catch enough caterpillars to feed their hungry chicks. When they are a little older, the babies will join the chorus of "chick-dee-dee."

C stands for Chickadee, Maine's special bird.
In woods and meadows, her song can be heard.
She dines on suppers of insects and seeds,
which she finds in feeders, gardens, and weeds.

Long ago, large ships moved by sails. In those days, when sailors left Boston for Maine, they were going "Down East," even though, on a map, it looked as though they were going up. The sailors meant they would sail to the east and "down wind," in the direction the wind was blowing, which would always bring them to the harbors and islands of Maine. We still use the phrase "Down East" to mean going up into the state, even though today we're more likely to go in cars than in wooden sailing ships.

D is for Down East,
another name for Maine.
When you know that east means east, but down means up,
the mystery of the name becomes plain.

The battle of the *Enterprise* and the *Boxer* was an exciting moment in Maine's history.

On September 5, 1813, during the War of 1812 with England, the American ship *Enterprise*, commanded by 28-year-old Lieutenant William Burrows, fought the British ship *Boxer*, commanded by 29-year-old Captain Samuel Blythe. In the Gulf of Maine off Monhegan Island, the ships fired at each other from close range for 45 minutes before the badly damaged *Boxer* surrendered to the Americans. The two young captains died during the battle and were buried side by side in Portland's Eastern Cemetery. Poems and stories have been written about how bravely the two captains and their crews fought.

Enterprise, which begins with the letter E,
was a brig that once sailed upon the sea.
The American warship battled the Boxer.
Both crews fought bravely, but the Enterprise outfoxed her.

More than 90% percent of Maine is covered in forests. No other state has such a high percentage of woodlands. In the early days, forests were full of eastern white pine, so it was a natural choice for our official state tree. The pinecone tassel is our state flower. The "Pine Tree State" is our nickname.

Thanks to the huge forests, Maine became a leading boat builder during the days of wooden ships. In fact, the first ship built in Maine was in 1607, 13 years before the Pilgrims landed in Plymouth. Because of their long, straight trunks, pine trees were ideal for building ships' masts.

Pine is used today to build houses and make paper. Nearly all of Maine's commercial forests are privately owned, mostly by large paper and lumber companies.

F stands for Forests,
with trees tall and straight.
The majestic eastern white pines
are the official trees of our state.

Ff

G g

Gulls are gregarious seabirds. They will eat just about anything: fish and shellfish if they can catch them, and also carrion, rubbish, tourists' picnics, and young birds. They often flock together on piers, pilings, or house-tops, facing into the wind.

Gulls are white, gray, and black with hooked bills, painted wings, round tails, and webbed feet. They lay brownish eggs in nests made of sea-weed and grass, which they build on rocky cliffs or by the shoreline. When you hear a gull's screech for the first time, you will never forget the sound.

G is for the graceful Gull.
It soars and swoops and glides
over beaches, bays, and rocky cliffs
above Maine's coastal tides.

The ocean is a vast hunting ground for nutritious food. Maine's fishermen pull up large numbers of fish in nets every day. Fish with fins make up 90% of Maine's catch; the other 10% are mollusks (clams, mussels and oysters) and crustaceans (lobsters, shrimp and crabs).

Fish are the oldest *vertebrates*, which are animals with backbones. They swam in ancient oceans 450 billion years ago. Today, there are 25,000 species of fish in the world.

A halibut can live to be 40 years old, and it can spawn as many as two million eggs at one time. The haddock has a dark blotch by its fins and can grow as long as 44 inches. A female herring can lay 50,000 eggs each year. The hake can grow to be four feet long and weigh 40 pounds.

H is for Halibut, Haddock, Herring, and Hake,
fish that swim in the ocean, not in a lake.
Fishermen drop their nets many miles out to sea,
to catch fish suppers for your family.

Island begins with the letter I.
If you were a bird flying high in the sky,
you'd see a spot of land with water all around.
In Maine's lakes and bays, many islands can be found.

More than 1,300 islands are anchored off the Maine coast. The name "Maine" probably originated when English explorers wanted to refer to the main-land rather than the many islands off our coast.

The islands in Casco Bay are called the Calendar Islands because early explorers counted as many as 365 of them—the same number of days on a calendar! Maine's largest island is Mount Desert, which is part of Acadia National Park.

Early English settlers often chose to live on islands away from the Native Americans and the harsher mainland winters. Some of those islands, such as Swan's, Deer, Vinalhaven, and Monhegan, still have year-round resi-dents. Others, like Isle au Haut, have become summer vacation spots.

I i

Jack-in-the-pulpits grow along the edges of Maine's pine-filled woodlands. It is a North American perennial flower, which means that it blooms every year. The jack-in-the-pulpit has a green or brown hood over the flower spike that looks a little like the cap of a J. The shape reminded early settlers of preachers in pulpits. The jack-in-the-pulpit can grow to be three feet tall, but in Maine they are usually shorter. The fruit is a cluster of berries. Native Americans used the plant's thick, tuberous roots as food.

J looks a bit like a Jack-in-the-pulpit.
This wildflower grows in woods that are sunlit.
Its bloom reminds us of a preacher in a church,
who looks at his flock from a very high perch.

k K

Katahdin begins with the letter **K**.
The spot where night first turns into day
is a mountain in Maine a mile high—
stand here and be the first to see the sun rise in the sky.

Mount Katahdin is the state's tallest mountain and is located in north central Maine. It stands 5,268 feet above sea level, almost one mile high.Because Katahdin is so tall and so far east, it is the first place in the United States to glimpse the sun each morning. It is equally famous for its mountain trails and the spectacular views it offers. On very clear days you might see across 100 miles.

Katahdin sits near the beginning of the Appalachian National Scenic Trail, which follows the Appalachian Mountains for more than 2,000 miles to their end in Georgia.

The lobster is one of more than 26,000 types of crustaceans. A crustacean is an animal with a hard shell body. Lobsters have thick tails, stalked eyes, long antennae, and five pairs of legs.

Maine is the largest lobster-producing state in the nation. Fishermen catch lobsters in lobster pots, or traps, which are slatted cages with an opening covered by a funnel shaped net. When the lobster moves into the pot, the net catches them. Pilgrims wrote about netting lobsters eight feet long in the early 1600s. The largest lobster officially recorded weighed 45 pounds.

Old-timers in Maine cook their lobsters right on the rocks, boiling them in salt water and seaweed for extra flavor. While alive, lobsters are dark green, but, when boiled, they turn bright red.

L is for Lobster, a two-clawed crustacean
that lives among rocks in shallow parts of the ocean.
Buoys mark traps where lobsters are caught.
They are red when you eat them, but green in the pot.

Ll

M represents Maine and
its special animal, the moose,
who lives in marshes and woodlands
with birch trees and spruce.
Moose antlers and noses are very big.
Their legs are long and skinny;
they'll never dance a jig.

The Moose is the tallest animal living in north America's forests and the largest member of the deer family. You can find him in moist, wooded areas, where he eats small shrubs, trees and aquatic plants in summer, and tree bark and lichens in winter. Early on summer mornings, you may see a moose swim across a quiet lake, taking his morning exercise. Or, you may hear him lumbering through marshlands.

The moose is dark brown, with a brown muzzle, heavy mane, and a large fold of loose skin called a dewlap that hangs beneath his neck. A moose can grow to be nine feet long, five-and-one-half-feet high at the shoulder, and weigh as much as 1,800 pounds. Every spring he sheds his massive antlers and grows a new set.

Moose share their marshes and wood-land homes with beavers, bobcats, black bears, raccoons, rabbits, porcupines, deer, and foxes.

Pronounced "chow-dah" by the people with the best recipes, New England Clam Chowder is one of the tastiest meals served in Maine. Chowders are eaten as enthusiastically today as they were by our early settlers.

Although New England Clam Chowder is the most famous of the thick, milky soups, New Englanders also love corn chowders and fish chowders, especially on nights when a nor'easter is blowing and all the world seems white.

All true New England chowders contain milk, onions, potatoes, and pork scraps. There is no one-and-only genuine way to make chowder. Many Down East cooks use special recipes that have been handed down in their families for generations. When one calls for fish stock or clam "liquor" (liquid), that's a clue that the recipe is old.

N stands for New England Clam Chowder,
a wonderful soup that all Yankees prefer.
Potatoes, onions, and clams simmer in the pot,
then the soup is served hot when the weather is not.

A canoe is a narrow, shallow boat that is usually pointed at both ends. Ancient people all around the world built canoes, but the ones made by our Maine natives were different. The wooden canoe frame was covered with pieces of birch bark sewn together. The seams were made watertight with pitch. In the nineteenth century, the Penobscots created a canvas canoe similar in design.

The Penobscots called the spot on the Penobscot River where they wintered every year Old Town, and the name was translated into English. In the late 1800s, three brothers with the last name of Gray ran a hardware store in Old Town. In 1898, behind their store, they built a canoe using traditional Penobscot methods. This was the start of the Old Town Indian Canoe Company, which later dropped "Indian" from its name. Every year the company builds more than 45,000 canoes and kayaks.

O stands for Old Town Canoe.
I can canoe, can you?
In a narrow, shallow boat over waters we paddle,
going much faster than on a horse with a saddle.

Maine has been blessed with generations of extraordinary people. Innovative natives, enterprising explorers, and courageous settlers helped make Maine such a special place.

Archeologists say that tribes that formed the Algonquin Nation roamed the coastline and woodlands of Maine for 10,000 years before European explorers and settlers arrived. The earliest European settlers were Pilgrims who came from England. The Scots-Irish and a number of Quakers, or Friends, from other colonies soon followed them. In the 1740s, Germans settled in Waldoboro and then the Irish moved to York, Lincoln, and Cumberland counties. French missionaries and traders controlled much of Maine's territory until 1759, when England won control of the land. French Canadians came to work in Maine's textile, shoe, and paper mills. Later, Finns, Russians, Poles, and Italians arrived. Swedish immigrants established New Sweden in northern Aroostook County in the 1870s.

P stands for Penobscots, and Passamaquoddies,
the first people of Maine.
They hunted, fished, trapped game,
and gave many mountains, rivers, and lakes their names.

Q is for Quoddy Lighthouse, a friend that stands beside the sea,
warning of dangers so ships sail worry-free.
On top of its tower burns a bright light
that cuts through the fog and the dark of the night.

Quoddy Lighthouse is officially known as West Quoddy Head Light and is located just south of Lubec. It is one of 63 light-houses guarding the coast of Maine.

Our oldest lighthouse is Portland Head Light. Commissioned by George Washington in 1790, it protects Maine's largest harbor. West Quoddy was built 18 years later, and then rebuilt in 1858 with a 49-foot tower. It stands on the easternmost point of the United States, to guide sailors around Campobello Island and the dangerous Bay of Fundy waters. West Quoddy was the first lighthouse to use a fog bell.

For hundreds of years lighthouse keep-ers kept the lights burning and foghorns blasting during storms and fogs. Now, the lights are automated and families no longer live on the isolated points of land to maintain the lights.

Q q

Maine is renowned for its magnificent gray rock-bound coast. During the nineteenth century, many islands off the coast were quarried for their granite rocks. "Stone-sloopers" carried huge blocks of granite to cities where they would be used to build capitol buildings, museums, and monuments.

Rocks also lie under much of Maine's interior. Only 3% of Maine's land area is used to grow crops, thanks to the rocky fields and hills.

A special kind of rock found in Maine is the state gem, the tourmaline. This semi-precious stone is glassy and can be black, red, green, brown, purple, or blue. Tourmalines make beautiful jewelry and are also used in electronic instruments.

The word Rock begins with the letter R.
Maine's rocks have made the state a star.
Photographers film them, painters paint them
as the rocks churn waves into foam.
These rocks are where puffins, porpoises, sea birds, and seals
come to make their home.

S swirls and slithers like the curves of Seashells.
Round, oval, conical, or crescent-shaped, painted with a palette of pastels,
shells are homes to miniature animals, who carry them on their backs.
If you look closely at the sand, you'll see their tiny tracks.

S s

Quahogs, conch, and cockle shells. Tritons, turbans, and thatchers. Barnacles, angel wings, harp shells, and mussels. Seahorses, urchins, and snails. Look for these shells on the beach or in a rock-bound pool of water, especially after a storm, when waves have churned the ocean floor and tossed its contents onto the beach.

The sand dollar is a special seashell you might find in Maine. A small animal lives inside the round, flat shell, which looks like an old-fashioned silver dollar stamped with a star. Tiny, hairlike spines cover the shell. Tinier hairs on the spines wave and the movement pulls food to the spines. A sticky, syrupy liquid from the spines flows down the grooves on the sand dollar's body and runs right into the animal's mouth, bringing it its evening meal.

The ocean has waves and tides. Waves are caused by the wind blowing over an open stretch of water. Waves that break along the coast may have been caused by storms far away in the middle of the ocean, or by local winds breezing over the beach.

Tides are the alternating rise and fall of the sea's surface caused by the gravitational pull of the sun and moon. Twice a day, ocean water creeps up on beaches. When the tide is high, the waves invite wave jumping and swimming. Then, hours later, the tide will leave the beach wide-open for building sand castles.

Tides follow the moon's cycle of 28 days. When the sun and moon line up perfectly, the high tides are the highest and the low are the lowest; these are called spring tides. When the sun and the moon are at right angles, tidal ranges are lowest; these are called neap tides.

T is for the Tide,
which comes and goes along Maine's ocean side.
In and out…in and out…the salty waters pour
while the sun and moon play tug of war.

The University of Maine starts with **U**.
Here, students called "Black Bears" dress in blue.
A University is a place where big kids go
to learn about everything they should know.

The University of Maine gave our nation the most famous college song. Singer Rudy Vallee made the University's "Stein Song" famous worldwide in the 1920s. The university mascot is the black bear, a big, formidable animal that roams in Maine's woods.

The University of Maine is a land-grant university founded in Orono just after the Civil War. In 1868, two teachers and 12 students launched the university. Now more than 11,000 students attend classes on the Orono campus and a total of 30,000 students are enrolled in the university system, which has eight campuses throughout the state.

Maine also has fine private colleges, among them Colby, Bowdoin, and Bates.

U u

V is for Vacationland,
     another name for Maine.
       This is a place where visitors come
by boat, bus, car, or plane.
      They swim, sail, ski, hike, and climb,
        and then go home after having a wonderful time!

The first tourist might have been Italian explorer Giovanni da Verrazzano, who sailed our way in 1524 on behalf of the king of France. Many others from different nations soon followed him. By the second half of the nineteenth century, Maine had become a place where summer visitors came to rest, relax, go boating, and enjoy nature.

At the turn of the last century, Bar Harbor was a playground for very wealthy vacationers. Families with names like Rockefeller, Vanderbilt, Morgan, and Pulitzer built "cottages" (really, large mansions) by the sea, where they entertained their friends and enjoyed their families.

Vacationers come here to swim, sail, or paddle across the waves. They build sand castles on beaches, climb rocky ledges overlooking the sea, and cast fishing lines in streams and lakes.

A Windjammer is a large wooden ship with tall, billowy sails. Windjammers used to carry passengers and cargo all around the world.

The earliest Maine-built ship sailed in 1607. After the mid-1700s, Maine's ship builders began to experiment with different riggings, or arrangements of ropes and sails. The fastest, most beautiful, and shortest-lived of the great sailing ships was the clipper ship, named because it sailed so fast it could "clip off" the miles. Clippers were soon replaced by Windjammers, which were larger and could carry more cargo. Steamships outmoded Windjammers in the mid-nineteenth century.

Whales are large sociable animals. Their bodies are shaped like fish, but their fins are shaped like paddles. Whales breathe through blowholes on top of their heads, and you might see one spout before it slides under the water, or as it glides above the waves.

W is for Windjammer and W is for Whale.
Over waves they slide and glide, sometimes side by side.
Windjammers are big ships that travel with sails,
while whales are big mammals that flop and flip their tails.

No one knows the exact number of ships that sank at sea or were wrecked on Maine's rocks during blinding storms, but there were many of them. Most were ruined in the days of wooden ships when sailors had only compasses and the stars to guide them. The skeletons of some ancient wooden hulls and some more recent iron ships can be spotted along the coast when the tide is low.

A "piece of eight" is an old Spanish silver coin. Between 400 and 500 years ago, Spanish treasure ships sailed from Mexico to Spain and pirates tried to capture them because they carried chests full of gold, jewels, and pieces of eight. According to legend, pirates sailed into Maine's isolated coves and harbors to bury their treasure.

X marks the spot
where ships met their fate.
Wrecks hide treasures that time forgot—
perhaps even pirates' pieces of eight!

Y is for York, the Grand Old Duke of York,
who had 10,000 men
and marched them up a very high hill
and marched them down again.
He also gave his name
to the oldest town in Maine.

The province of Maine was organized with a charter signed by England's King Charles I in 1639. Settlers established its capital two years later on the spot where York now stands, although they called the settlement Gorgeana. Later it was renamed York, after the Duke of York, who was a famous soldier.

Although it is a small, sleepy village now, York has played an important role in America's history. Incorporated in 1641, York is the oldest chartered English city in North America. In the late 1600s, it was the site of a tragic Indian massacre. Later, during the American Revolution, the people of York defied the British government and held their own version of a Boston Tea Party. They dumped imported tea into the harbor because they also felt the British Parliament had unlawfully taxed the tea.

York has the oldest religious parish in our state.

The Emerson-Wilcox House

The John Hancock Wharf and Warehouse.

The George Marshall Store.

The First Parish Church.

The Old Gaol.

Because so much of Maine lies far from cities, there are many places to sit outside and watch the sky fill with stars.

Stars are special objects in the sky that are millions of miles away. If you are especially lucky, on a dark night in Maine you'll be able to spot the northern lights, or *aurora borealis*, which are streamers of lights that paint the night sky with color.

An observatory is a place where you can learn more about the stars in the sky. The Maynard F. Jordan Planetarium and Observatory at the University of Maine in Orono, and the Southworth Planetarium at the University of Southern Maine teach about the stars and planets. Maine's oldest observatory is the Portland Observatory on Munjoy Hill. It was actually built as a signal tower rather than a place to watch the stars. In 1807, Lemuel Moody built the tower to spot ships heading for Portland Harbor. It is the only signal tower remaining in the United States.

Z is for Zillion,
　　　the number of stars in the sky.
They seem close enough to touch
　　　on a dark night in July.

A Lobster Pot of Facts

1. Who were the earliest people to live in Maine?

2. Which Maine city is the oldest English-chartered city in North America?

3. When did Maine become a state?

4. What other state claimed Maine's lands for many years?

5. What is Maine's capital? What happens there?

6. What is Maine's state bird? What song does she sing?

7. What is Maine's state animal? How big is he?

8. What is Maine's state tree? How is it related to our state flower?

9. What is an island and how many islands does Maine have?

10. Where does the sun first rise in North America every day?

11. What is special about the lobster's color?

12. What are two special facts about Old Town?

13. How many lighthouses guard Maine's coast? Which is the oldest?

14. How many miles of coastline does Maine have?

15. How much land in Maine is used to grow crops?

16. How much land in Maine is covered in forests?

17. Can you name some special shells you can find on one of Maine's beaches?

18. How important is fishing to Maine?

Answers

1. Members of the Algonquin nation set up their homes, hunted, fished and trapped animals here in what would become Maine perhaps as long as 10,000 years ago. Among the tribes were the Penobscots and Passamaquoddies, who gave many of our mountains, lakes, and rivers their names. European settlers arrived in the early 1600s.

2. Although today it looks like a small, sleepy village, York is our continent's oldest English city.

3. Maine entered the Union on March 15, 1820 as our country's 23rd state.

4. Maine was a part of Massachusetts from 1691 until 1820.

5. Augusta is Maine's capital. It is the city where the governor lives, where our elected representatives make laws, and where our state's Supreme Court rules on important law cases.

6. Maine's state bird is the chickadee. She sings her song "chick-dee-dee" in the woods and meadows here in Maine.

7. Maine's state animal is the moose. Male moose can grow to be nine feet long, five-and-a-half feet high at the shoulder, and weigh as much as 1,800 pounds.

8. Maine's state tree is the eastern white pine. This tree has been very important in our shipbuilding and timber industries. In fact, it is so important to Maine that our state flower is the pine cone and tassel.

9. An island is a body of land surrounded by water. Maine has over 1,300 islands off its coast.

10. The sun first touches North America every day on Mt. Katahdin, which is nearly a mile high.

11. Live lobsters are a dark green color when they are caught, but when they are boiled they become bright red.

12. Natives from the Algonquin nation, who returned to this spot year after year to spend the winter, founded old Town. For the last 100 years, Old Town is also the place where Old Town Canoes are made.

13. Sixty-three lighthouses guard the coast of Maine, warning ships and sailors of dangerous rocks or waterways. The oldest lighthouse is Portland Head Light.

14. Maine's coastline extends for 367 miles, but it is deeply indented by bays, inlets and river estuaries. If all these are measured, the shoreline of Maine is 3,478 miles long.

15. Farms cover only 3% of Maine's total land, thanks to the rocky soil here. When a tourist asked one early farmer what he raised on his farm, he grunted and said, "Rocks."

16. Forests cover 90% of Maine's land. Industries that relate to the forests—timbering, paper, and Christmas trees—are very important in Maine's economy.

17. Maine's beaches can be treasure troves for shells: quahogs, conch, cone, clam, cockle, tritons, turbans, thatchers, barnacles, angel wings, harp shells, mussels, razor clams, spindle shells, snail shells, sea urchins, sand dollars, and starfish.

18. Fishing is a very important industry and way of life in Maine. Our fishermen pull up a tremendous number of fish in their nets every day. Many people who visit Maine come to eat fresh fish dinners.

Cynthia Furlong Reynolds

Cynthia Furlong Reynolds is an award-winning journalist who set out on a quest for lilting rhymes and intriguing X, Y, and Z words when she began to write this book. Her byline has appeared in many magazines and on her first book: *Our Hometown: America's History as Seen Through the Eyes of a Midwestern Village* (also by Sleeping Bear Press). Her ancestors started coming to Maine in the 1600s; many of them settled on islands off the coast and became gardeners, sailors, and ship captains who told wonderful stories about the old days "Down East." Cynthia was born in Portland, into a family that would eventually include four girls. She now lives with her husband, Mark, and their three children, enjoying the country life with two dogs and one Maine garden snake.

Jeannie Brett

Jeannie Brett has lived in New England her entire life and in Maine for 24 years. She grew up in the coastal town of Hingham, Massachusetts, where she developed a passion for animals and the outdoors that continues today. Jeannie studied at the School of the Museum of Fine Arts in Boston and at the Minneapolis College of Art and Design. Jeannie lives in York, Maine with her husband, Greg, and their three children, Gregory, Sophie, and Lee. They share their home with two horses, two bunnies, three enormous cats, and a wonderful old Newfoundland.